Creative Coping Skills
for Children

Creative Coping Skills for Children

Emotional Support through Arts and Crafts Activities

WRITTEN AND ILLUSTRATED BY
BONNIE THOMAS

Jessica Kingsley Publishers
London and Philadelphia

First published in 2009
by Jessica Kingsley Publishers
116 Pentonville Road
London N1 9JB, UK
and
400 Market Street, Suite 400
Philadelphia, PA 19106, USA

www.jkp.com

Library of Congress Cataloging in Publication Data
Thomas, Bonnie, 1971-
   Creative coping skills for children : emotional support through arts and crafts activities /
Bonnie Thomas ; illustrated by Bonnie Thomas.
      p. cm.
   ISBN 978-1-84310-921-1 (pb : alk. paper) 1. Children--Life skills guides. 2. Child development. 3.
Emotions in children. 4. Creative activities and seat work. I. Title.
   HQ767.9.T485 2009
   155.4'1246--dc22

                                                               2008043850

British Library Cataloguing in Publication Data
A CIP catalogue record for this book is available from the British Library

ISBN 978 1 84310 921 1

Printed and bound in Great Britain by
Athenaeum Press, Gateshead, Tyne and Wear

Contents

Introduction

I have to admit I rarely read the introductions to books. I am usually too eager to move on to the content or I am really short on time. I'm an official Introductions Skipper. But as the writer of this book I can hardly skip this particular intro.

That being said, this book came about for one main reason—I wanted to write a book that helps both parents *and* professionals teach children coping skills in unique and engaging ways. There are some wonderful parenting books and other media that help parents teach their children coping skills. There are also some professional texts for therapists, social workers, teachers, etc. that address children and coping skills. But where are the books written for both parents and professionals combined? Where is that one simple text that addresses us as adults wanting to help children? I had trouble finding such a resource and that is what inspired me to write my own.

The ideas in this book come from my experience as a parent as well as my experience as a child and family therapist. I have worked with children as young as three and through the teen years.

Whether you are a parent, a professional, or both, this book is designed to help you teach a child some coping skills. Many children are dynamic, imaginative, and creative. Some children are much more cerebral and literal. Therefore, some interventions in this book are constructed around arts and crafts activities, where other interventions include workbooks, coloring pages, incentive charts, and prescribed rituals. Whatever the need for your child, there are many interventions in this book to try.

A Note about Materials Used in these Projects

Many of the projects listed in this book contain a materials list. As a mother and counselor (with no budget for therapy supplies) I try hard to be frugal in gathering supplies for projects. I also try to be mindful and use recycled materials when possible.

The majority of the supplies used for these projects were either donated or found for free. I have listed ways I have accrued such supplies to help you do the same.

- Check your local recycling center for boxes, jars, wood, and various recycled goods. Some recycling centers even have an area put aside for items that are still usable, such as games (I use many game pieces in craft projects) and containers.

- Let friends and family know that you are collecting supplies such as fabric, yarn, clothing (cut the clothing into fabric squares), discarded jewelry (strip it for the beads and charms), buttons, and any re-usable arts and crafts supplies they no longer want or need.

- Let friends with small children know you would be glad to take on those little plastic figurines and loose game pieces that are usually at the bottom of the toy box. My peers also know I do play therapy with children and therefore they sometimes contact me before they donate any toys, puzzles, or games.

- Check those "free" piles of items that are put at the end of people's driveways after they have had a yard sale.

- Check your local library for free magazines (many libraries have a section set aside for magazine exchanges). Magazines are great for collage and altered art projects.

- Collect paint samples from hardware stores. Paint samples are great to have on hand for collages, paper scraps, and Reminder Rings (instructions included in this book). Some hardware stores even have laminate samples for countertops, which are great for using in art projects.

- If you do need to purchase items, check a local dollar store first. Wooden clothespins are an item I purchase regularly, and these are cheaper at the dollar store than a department store.

A Note about Coping Skills

Children learn coping skills via various means. One way is by observing adults around them. Whatever your role is with a child, they surely know how you cope with life's stressors. Do you tense up? Yell? Swear? Take it in your stride? Take deep breaths? Stop breathing? One of the easiest ways to help a child learn some healthy coping skills is to use them yourself and even voice it out loud when you are using them. For example, "I'm really angry that person pulled out in front of me. I'm going to take a deep breath and let it out."

Children also learn coping skills by observing how people and characters cope in the media. How do the characters in your child's favorite TV shows, movies, and books handle stress? If the characters are making poor choices and present with poor coping skills, is this affecting your child's perception of how to deal with their own feelings? This a great conversation topic for adults and children. Simply ask "Who is your favorite character in _____? How does that character act when he or she is upset? What do you think about that character's reaction? Does that reaction make things easier or harder for that character?"

In the end, however, children will learn coping skills via trial and error. Let your children, clients, students, etc. know that coping skills are a learning process and that some skills will work great for one child, and maybe not so great for the next. You can present it as an experiment (for those scientifically minded children) or an adventure (for those sensory seeking children) or a scavenger hunt (for those curious children) or even as a security plan (for those anxious children). We all need to "try on" different coping skills and see how they fit.

Everybody has different needs when it comes to coping with life's stressors. Children are no different. Some children need quiet and soothing activities in order to calm down, where others need more physical activity or intense sensory input in order to calm their bodies and minds.

Part 1

Coping Skills
and Strategies

Coping Skills and Strategies: A Starting Point

Here are various coping interventions that you can review with a child. There are two separate lists here for your reference. The reason is that many children fall into one category or the other—the quieter calming interventions are for those childen who need a break from sensory stimuli in order to feel calm. The other list is for children who need to release energy and sensory stimuli in order to keep calm. Of course, many children will benefit from interventions from both lists, but the lists have been separated for clarity. It's a great starting place to assess which coping skills the child has already tried and which have or haven't worked. You can also use these lists to find new coping interventions that the child may be willing to try.

If you are a counselor or other professional working with a child, you can incorporate these lists into a child's goals. For example, the child could try ten coping interventions from either list and rate them on a scale of 1 to 5 to determine which ones were most successful at helping them cope with stressors. From there you can create a coping plan.

When using these lists with a child you can have them draw smiley faces next to the strategies they have tried and an exclamation point or other symbol next to the ones they are willing/wanting to try.

The lists follow on separate pages to allow for easier photocopying. Instructions for items marked with an * are included in the book.

Quiet and soothing coping interventions

- Take a soothing bath
- Talk to a friend
- Meditate
- Pray
- Play some quiet relaxing music
- Hug a stuffed animal or pillow
- Create something
- Make a favorite recipe (with adult supervision)
- Remind yourself that everyone has bad days now and then
- Read an inspiring book
- Curl up in a warm blanket
- Think of five things you are grateful for
- Sip some relaxing tea or warm milk
- Soak your feet in warm soapy water—close your eyes and relax
- Write in a journal
- Trace a finger labyrinth*
- Listen to some meditation or visualization stories
- Knit
- Doodle
- Build a fort with pillows and blankets and hide inside
- Turn your situation and feelings into a comic strip
- Take five deep breaths
- Think of what has gone right today
- Blow some bubbles

- Rock in a rocking chair
- Reflect on a funny moment or funny joke
- Color a mandala* or other picture
- Pat your dog or cat and tell them about your day
- Stretch your muscles slowly and gently
- Look at a Thinga-ma-find*
- Run your fingers through a Box of Blops*

Physical and sensory input interventions

- Take a five minute brisk walk
- Do some sit-ups
- Play with play dough or clay
- Chew on some ice
- Chew bubble gum
- Suck on sour or spicy candy
- Do something you enjoy
- Play some favorite music loudly
- Sing loudly
- Hug a stuffed animal or pillow as hard as you can
- Create something
- Knead some bread or pizza dough
- Squeeze your muscles and then relax them
- Massage your feet
- Scribble on paper—see how much of the page you can cover
- Sip a hot drink (not so hot you burn yourself, of course) or a really cold drink
- Write your feelings down in a journal
- Tear and crumple up a phone book or paper (but ask an adult first if the item you want to tear is ok)
- Make a rubber band ball
- Wrap yourself up tightly in a blanket (make sure you can breathe!)
- Take a shower
- Fling rubber bands at the wall
- Scream into a pillow
- Melt an ice cube in your hands
- Do some push-ups

- Run your fingers through a Box of Blops*
- Blow up balloons and then let all the air out by letting them go
- Make a picture by poking holes into the paper with a pencil
- Make an aluminum foil ball or sculpture
- Make silly faces—scrunch up all those face muscles

Putting Words to Feelings

Children need the vocabulary to define how they feel. They are much less likely to feel overwhelmed if they can put words to their emotions. Find "teachable moments" to talk to children about feelings in general. This will help children build their vocabulary around self-expression. Voice your own feelings so they can hear and make the connection between feelings and words.

The following workbook is a tool to help you communicate with a child about some basic feelings.

My Book about Feelings

This book belongs to _____

Do any of these things make you feel happy? If so, circle them!

Family   Hugs

            Petting a friendly dog or cat

Swimming   Bedtime stories

                Birthday parties

            Seeing a rainbow

                            Playing with my friend

    Ice cream sundaes   Getting mail

Blue skies   The smell of grass

    Holidays   Painting   Candy

            When someone tells me "Good job!"

Playing "tag"   Building something

                Having a pillow fight

What else makes you feel

HAPPY?

Create a Happy Story

Once upon a time there was a very happy _____. Why was the _____ so happy? Well, today was a special day, a day for celebrating _____. This is how the _____ celebrated this day:

_____

_____

_____

Sounds fun, doesn't it? Draw a picture of the _____ celebrating this special day.

Why are they happy?

Do any of these things make you feel sad? If so, circle them!

Seeing someone cry

Breaking a favorite toy

Having a time out

When a pet dies

When someone picks on me

When no one wants to play with me

When I miss my mom, dad, or someone close to me

When a relative dies

When someone yells at me

When someone else gets more attention than me

When I've lost something

When someone isn't friendly to me

What else makes you feel

SAD?

Create a Sad Story

Once upon a time there was a very sad _____.

The _____ was sad because

_____

_____

_____

_____

Oh, that is sad! The _____ was so sad that tears filled up the whole _____.

Draw a picture of all those tears.

Why are they sad?

_____

_____

_____

_____

_____

_____

_____

_____

_____

_____

_____

Do any of these things make you feel mad? If so, circle them!

When your brother or sister plays with your friends

When someone won't share with you

When someone cuts in front of line

When you get blamed for something you didn't do

When you don't win a game

When you don't understand your homework

Getting up too early in the morning

When other kids call you names

When you drop your ice cream on the ground

When someone says they'll visit you and they don't keep their promise

When recess is over

What else makes you feel

MAD?

Create a Mad Story

Once upon a time there was a very angry _____. I knew it was angry because smoke was coming out of its _____. I could tell it was furious because its _____ was turning the color of _____. I could tell it was enraged and aggravated and irritated because it was stomping its _____.

Draw a picture showing why the _____ was so mad!

Why are they mad?

_____

_____

_____

_____

_____

_____

_____

_____

_____

_____

_____

Draw something scary!

This wizard has captured the scary thing from your picture. He has shrunk it and put it in this bottle.

Where in your body do you feel different feelings? Follow the color code and color in the places where you feel each feeling.

Happy = Pink

Sad = Blue

Mad = Red

Scared = Black

Finger Labyrinths

Labyrinths are ancient patterns that have often been used in meditation. There are many forms of labyrinths, many of which are "walking labyrinths." If you ever find a walking labyrinth near you, try walking one with a child. Many children love the winding paths of labyrinths. They also tend to rush through them. (I have been told by labyrinth owners that this is typical. Children need less "closure" than adults and they will walk or run the labyrinth at the pace that works for them.) To find a labyrinth near you, access the World-Wide Labyrinth Locator at www.wwll.veriditas.labyrinthsociety.org. You may be surprised to find how many labyrinths are near you!

There are other forms of labyrinths that include handheld wooden labyrinths that you "trace" with a special tool. There are also finger labyrinths, such as the one on the following page, that you follow with your finger. The goal of this labyrinth is to trace your finger from the outside of the labyrinth to the center, *and back out again.* Your finger traces the white path—try to do so without lifting your finger.

start here

Trace the path of the labyrinth with your finger. Follow the path to the center of the labyrinth AND back out again without lifting your finger.

Thinga-ma-finds

Thinga-ma-finds are a wonderful tool to have on hand when working or living with children. A Thinga-ma-find is a jar filled with dry rice and trinkets. The child turns and manipulates the jar in order to reveal different objects hidden in the rice. This can be a soothing activity for a child who needs a few minutes of transition or quiet time. The activity provides sensory input as well as distraction, both of which can be calming for children.

Materials

- A plastic bottle or jar
- Rice
- Various trinkets, buttons, charms, odds and ends

Directions

- Place all of the items and rice into the plastic bottle/jar
- Cap the bottle/jar and shake the contents

Variation

Instead of placing the objects and rice in a bottle/jar, place it all in a plastic container with a lid. Have the child sort through the rice with their hands to find the hidden objects.

Reminder Rings

Reminder Rings are cards attached to a string or key chain that remind the child of some coping skills he or she can use. They are a good substitute for when you can't be there to remind the child of the skills they have. For example, a child who gets separation anxiety may find these useful to have in a backpack for bus rides to school or to use during the school day.

Materials

- Several small pieces of cardstock paper (individual paint samples from a hardware store also work well)
- Markers and pen
- Stickers, stamps, or pictures cut from magazines
- Hole punch
- A key ring or string
- Beads (optional)

Directions

- Have a discussion with the child about coping skills they use that have worked.
- Have the child pick out the color cards they would like—they will need one card per coping skill.
- Write down a coping skill on each card.
- Have the child decorate their cards.
- Punch a hole in the upper left corner of each card.

- Attach the cards to the key ring, or tie them together with a loop of string. You can thread beads onto the string if desired.

Now the child can carry these portable reminders with them easily. Many of the children I work with have kept these in a small pocket of their backpacks at school. Some children have made more than one set so they can have one at a parent's house and one at school. These cards can be kept as discreet or "out in the open" as the child wants. Younger children tend to flaunt them whereas older children usually choose to keep them private.

Support Bracelets and Necklaces

Children can make these bracelets and necklaces as a reminder of people who care about them and support them, as well as passions and interests that sustain them. They are handy for those difficult moments when the child needs support but has to move forward on his or her own (e.g. first day of school) They are also handy for celebrating a rite of passage, especially if the child is struggling with separartion and anxiety.

Materials

- Paper and pencil
- A variety of beads that include a mix of colors, shapes, and letters
- Beading string

Directions

- Make a list of all the people, pets, and supports the child has for helping them cope in tough times. They can list family members, friends, pets, religion, guardian angels, imaginary friends, a community helper who is friendly to them, hopes or dreams, a teacher, etc. If the child has a passion for something (such as sports, music, journaling) they can list this also.

- Have the child pick out a bead to represent each item they listed. For example, a child might choose a red bead to represent a grandmother who likes the color red; or if you have animal shaped beads, the child can use one to represent a pet. The child chooses as many beads as they need to represent all of their natural supports.

They could also use alphabet beads to spell out a word that reminds them of someone supportive or of a coping skill that works well for them.

- Have the child create a bracelet or necklace from these beads.

When complete, the child can wear their bracelet/necklace during difficult or celebratory times. For example:

- First day of school
- During a hospitalization
- Preparing for a rite of passage
- Doing a class presentation
- Summer camp.

Variation

Children enjoy making these for others as well as wearing them. Therefore, children can make these bracelets/necklaces as a way to show support to someone else. Reaching out and helping others can be a soothing activity for children as it gives them a way to help and be in control of the situation (even if it's a small part they can control). Consider helping a child make a bracelet/necklace for a loved one during other times of separation such as business trips, rehab, or heading off to war.

Support Bracelets and Necklaces: One Step Further

This activity is basically the same as the last, except that in this version you will be making charms to represent each support rather than choosing beads.

Materials

- Paper and pencil
- Craft plastic for shrinking
- Scissors
- Hole punch
- Permanent markers, both thin and thick tipped
- Parchment paper
- An oven
- Beads
- Beading string or other bracelet/necklace material
- 7mm jump rings (optional—these can be fixed to the charms for easier attachment to bracelet/necklace)

Directions

- Read and review the directions for the shrinking plastic.

- Make a list of all the people, pets, and supports the child has for helping them cope in tough times. They can list family members, friends, pets, religion, guardian angels, imaginary friends, a community helper who is friendly to them, hopes or dreams, a teacher, etc. If the child has a passion for something (such as sports, music, journaling) they can list this also.

- Pre-cut pieces of plastic into various shapes without sharp edges (circles, rounded squares, heart shapes, flower shapes, etc.). Make sure these shapes are about three times larger than the shape you will want for a charm (the plastic shrinks in the oven).

- Use a hole punch to make two adjacent holes at the tops of the charms (if you are using jump rings you only need to punch one hole). Two holes will ensure that the charm will stay flat on the wrist/neck once strung.

- Have the child use the permanent markers to decorate and color the charms.

- When the child has finished decorating the charms, preheat the oven according to the directions for the shrinking plastic (this is usually to about 250 degrees).

- Place some parchment paper on a cooking sheet, then place the charms on the parchment paper. Bake the charms in the oven till they curl up and then shrink and become flat again.

- Remove the charms from the oven and allow them to cool.

- In the meantime, have the child pick out beads to fill in the spaces between the charms on the bracelet/necklace.

- When the charms have cooled, have the child create their bracelet/necklace with an alternating pattern of beads and charms.

Now the child has a visible reminder of their own natural supports, which they can wear, or hang someplace special, or give to someone else as a gift.

Stepping Stones and Power Pathways

Children can become overwhelmed by goals. If we facilitate breaking goals down into smaller steps, it makes it easier for the child to see that several smaller successes are easier to accomplish than one big goal all at once.

Stepping stones and power pathways are charts that help break down one big goal into several smaller goals. The child can see the "steps" to reaching his or her goals, or "steps" to gaining power in his or her new skill.

Materials

- Paper and pencil
- Pen
- Markers

Directions

- Have a discussion with the child about a goal he or she is working on.
- Brainstorm all of the steps the child needs to take to reach that goal.
- Put the steps in simple, sequential order.
- Now draw stepping stones on paper. Write the steps onto the stones in sequential order.
- Have the child decorate around the stepping stones.

- What is the child's reward for meeting this goal? Have them draw the reward at the end of the path.

- Use this as a visual aid to guide the child on what they need to do next to accomplish the goal.

On the following pages are some stepping stone charts you can photocopy for your own use.

My goal is: _____

STEP 1

STEP 2

START!

STEP 3

STEP 4

STEP 5

FINISH!

GOAL MET!!!
My reward:

Goal: _____

STEP 1

STEP 2

STEP 3

STEP 4

STEP 5

FINISH!

GOAL MET!!!
My reward:

STEP 2

STEP 1

STEP 3

STEP 4

My goal:

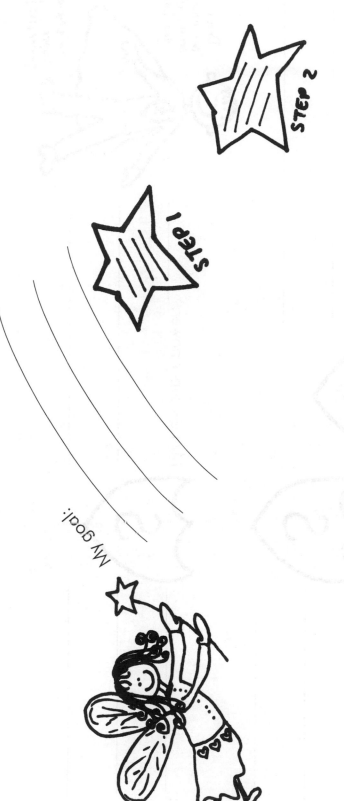

GOAL MET!!!
My reward:

This power pathway belongs to: _____

My goal: _____

Step 1: _____

Step 2: _____

Step 3: _____

Step 4: _____

My new super power: _____

Draw long hair on me if you like!

Girls have super power, too!

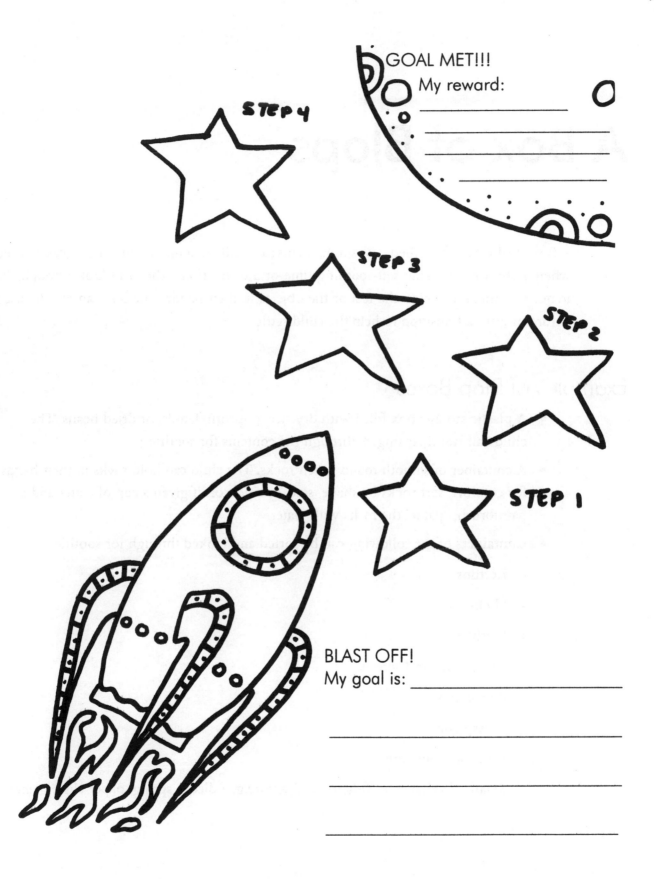

GOAL MET!!!
My reward:

_____
_____
_____
_____

STEP 4

STEP 3

STEP 2

STEP 1

BLAST OFF!
My goal is: _____

_____
_____
_____

A Box of Blops

A Box of Blops is a box filled with similar items for a child to look through. These can be used when a child needs some self-soothing time or a distraction—they can look through the items, sort them, or enjoy the feel of the objects in their hands. The box can also be used before or after a transition to help the child settle.

Examples of Blop Boxes

- A plastic storage box filled with dry rice, popcorn, lentils, or dried beans. The child can run their fingers through the contents for soothing.

- A container of smooth round beach rocks. The child can hold rocks in their hands for comfort; sort rocks by shape, size, or color; or, if given a cup of water and a paintbrush, "paint" the rocks with water.

- Containers of the following can be sorted and looked through for soothing:
  - Buttons
  - Shells
  - Marbles
  - Nuts, bolts, and screws
  - Pom-poms
  - Glass gems
  - Semi-precious stones
  - Small miscellaneous "fidgets" and toys (e.g. a dice, a spring, paper clips, game pieces)

- A plastic storage container filled with sand. The child can simply run their fingers through the sand or use small figurines or cars/trucks to set up a little world for their toys.

I like to keep a few of these boxes around and occasionally change them. The children I work with enjoy looking through several different objects and exploring new boxes. However, if you work with a child who has some rigid behaviors and they need that one box to forever be available in your office, you'd best leave it there. Children with autism and developmental delays are not always happy about changes.

Mandalas

Mandalas are typically a circular design that are soothing to color or draw. Many mandalas are symmetrical, but some are not. Mandalas have a rich history in the spiritual and art worlds. Mandalas were mainly used to help people focus their attention in a meditative manner. There are many coloring books of mandalas on the market, and some internet sites such as http://www.freekidscoloring.com/pattern/mandala/ and http://www.coloring-kids.com/mandala-coloring-book-pages.html have free mandalas to print out and color. On the following pages are a few kid-friendly mandalas to color.

55

Power Animals

Many cultures/tribes embrace power animals or animal medicine, believing that animals have their own strengths that we can learn from. Some children enjoy claiming their own power animals for helping them through tough times. Although there are many methods of helping children discover their power animals, the simplest may be just talking to them about the skill or resource they need in order to feel more confident about facing current challenges. For example, a teenager wishing they had more motivation to get their school work done might choose a bee for their power animal, or a child who doesn't receive much nurturing at home may choose a bear.

Once a child knows which power animal is their own then they can practice visualizing the power animal helping them through difficult times. For example, the child who needs more nurturing could visualize him- or herself as a bear cub and imagine the mother bear snuggling up with them each night as they go to sleep.

Power Animals: One Step Further

If your child or client enjoys using power animals, you can take it further by doing the following:

- Make a power animal collage.

- Illustrate a power animal totem pole.

- Look at a book on animal medicine.

- Make a stuffed animal of the child's power animal.

- Make a power animal bracelet/necklace (see p.41–44; you could make a power animal charm using the shrinking plastic or you can find a bead of the power animal).

A child who resists change and transitions may do well with a snake for a power animal. Snakes remind us to "shed our skin" and accept change. The snake was made from recycled tights, buttons, and ribbon.

A snail is a great power animal for a child who is working on goals around impulsivity or hyperactivity. This snail was made from socks and cotton stuffing.

Coping Skills Tool Kit

A Coping Skills Tool Kit is a collection of diversions, distractions, reminders, and "fidgets" that are put together in one kit. The kit is custom-made for the child based on his or her individual needs. These kits are great to have on hand so that if the child starts to feel agitated or needs a break, they have a kit of their own from which to pick and choose some calming activities.

Materials

- A recycled coffee can or sturdy box with lid
- Papers
- Markers or crayons
- Glue and/or tape
- Stickers
- Individualized items for the contents, for example:
  - Sketch pad and drawing supplies
  - Uplifting and encouraging notes written by adults
  - Journal
  - Knitting supplies
  - Silly putty
  - A squishy ball for squeezing
  - Favorite quotes
  - A favorite perfume sample from a magazine

- A collection of items that are soothing to look at or hold (e.g. marbles or collector's cards)

- Crystals or special rocks

- A prayer or saint card

- A photo that cheers the child up

Directions

- Have the child decorate the outside of their container.

- Fill the container with items that will help them calm down or keep distracted.

A Pirate's Survival Guide

Many children these days are struggling with multiple challenges related to poverty, addictions, and family tension. It can be very difficult for children to put words to these experiences and even harder to express their needs and feelings around them. However, if you externalize their problems it can make it easier for them to do so. A Pirate's Survival Guide is a child-friendly tool to help children talk about how to cope with multiple challenges as well as express their feelings about them. It is geared to counselors working with children.

A Pirate's

Survival Guide

A Pirate's Survival Guide

Pirates had a lot to deal with.

Sometimes, just as a pirate got settled into a new port or village, it was time to pack up again and head back out to sea. Some of them moved often to increase their chances of finding treasure. Some pirates moved often if they were in hiding—the more places they moved to, the harder it was to find them.

What do you think it was like for a pirate to "be on the move" so much?

I think it must have been...

_____

_____

_____

What do you think were some advantages to moving often?

I think some advantages were...

_____

_____

_____

What do you think were some disadvantages to moving often?

I think some disadvantages were…

_____

_____

This is Scallywag Skip

Time to pack ye' olde suitcase again! Argh!

Scallywag Skip wants to know: "What would *you* do to survive moving so often?"

If I had to move a lot I would "survive" by…

_____

_____

Some pirate captains were notoriously cruel and crabby. What do you think it was like to live with a captain who was cruel and crabby?

I bet it was…

_____

_____

Draw a crabby pirate captain here.

If the pirate captain was being crabby, how do you think the pirates on the ship acted around him or her?

I bet the other pirates…

_____

_____

Scallywag Skip wants to know: "What would *you* do to survive living on a pirate ship with a crabby captain?"

I would survive living with a crabby captain by…

_____

_____

Many pirate ships were crowded with pirates and the things they needed to bring for the long journey, such as tools and food. Space was limited and there was little, if any, room for privacy.

This is called "living in tight quarters."

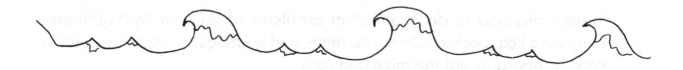

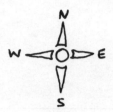

How many pirates can you draw on this ship?

Pirates also had to deal with other problems of living in tight quarters—things like lice, cockroaches, rats, mice, and bedbugs. Some ships even had cats on board to eat the mice and rats.

 Scallywag Skip wants to know: "How can I help keep lice from spreading quickly on the ship?"

_____

_____

Sometimes pirates drank too much rum, ale, and beer. How do you think they acted when they drank too much?

I think they acted...

_____

_____

_____

Draw a picture of a pirate who has had too much to drink.

Scallywag Skip wants to know: "What are some ways I could take care of myself and keep myself safe when others are drinking too much?"

Tips for Scallywag Skip:

_____

_____

_____

Many times, pirates were a bit rough with each other. Many pirates swore and some got into physical fights. What do you think it was like to be around so many unruly pirates?

I bet it was…

_____

_____

_____

What would you do if you were on a pirate ship and a fight broke out?

I would…

_____

_____

_____

72

Now, just for fun, pretend you are the captain of a pirate ship.

First, what is the name of your pirate ship?

My pirate ship is called…

_____

And what is your pirate name?

My name is Captain…

_____

What are the rules of your ship?

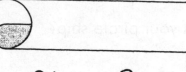

Ship Rules.....

1.

2.

3.

4.

5.

6.

7.

8.

9.

10.

Design your ship's flag.

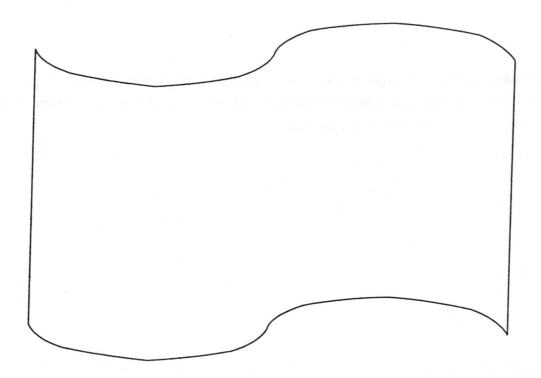

Taking Care of Me

Sometimes, even adults forget that simple strategies like eating healthily and getting enough sleep helps us regulate our moods and behavior much better. This is an activity book to help children learn and use some self-care skills.

This workbook belongs to _____

Taking Care of Me

There are many ways people can take good care of themselves. If you take good care of yourself, you will have a stronger foundation for coping with day-to-day stressors like frustration, disagreements with friends, problems at school, and so on.

One way to take good care of your body is to eat healthy foods and drink plenty of water. If you eat healthy foods, your body will be stronger to help fight germs and cope with stress.

Draw some healthy foods you like.

Another way you can take good care of yourself is to get a good night's sleep.

Check off any items that help you sleep better.

- ☐ Using a "white noise" machine
- ☐ Comfortable pajamas
- ☐ A clean bed
- ☐ A clean room
- ☐ Reading to yourself before bed
- ☐ Having someone read to you before bed
- ☐ Having a healthy bedtime snack
- ☐ Having a special blanket, toy, or doll to sleep with
- ☐ Snuggling with someone before bed
- ☐ Sucking your thumb
- ☐ Listening to music
- ☐ Having a bath or shower before bed
- ☐ Having some warm milk
- ☐ Wishing on a star
- ☐ Saying a prayer
- ☐ Getting a hug or kiss goodnight
- ☐ Turning on a nightlight
- ☐ Going to bed at a reasonable time
- ☐ Other _____

It is also important to get lots of physical activity to keep your body healthy and strong. Physical activity also helps you release tension and anger, and even makes you feel happier. What physical activities do you enjoy?

_____

_____

Draw a picture of you doing something physically active.

Do you enjoy any of these physical activities? If so, put a smiley face next to them.

- Climbing trees
- Playing hopscotch
- Throwing a football
- Doing yoga
- Chasing bubbles
- Building a fort
- Puddle jumping
- Swinging on the monkey bars
- Playing Frisbee
- Diving in the water
- Swinging high on a swing
- Building a snow sculpture
- Running through a sprinkler
- Going on a scavenger hunt
- Playing at the playground
- Playing freeze tag
- Stirring cookie dough
- Jumping on the bed
- Having a pillow fight
- Playing miniature golf

Self-care also means making sure your body is clean and that you take care of any illnesses and cuts or grazes you have.

Here are some reminders of ways to help your body stay clean and healthy:

- Brush your teeth at least twice a day—once when you wake up and once you when you go to bed. Use toothpaste and don't forget to brush your tongue, too.
- Cover your mouth and nose when you sneeze.
- Wash your hands after using the bathroom or blowing your nose.
- Check for ticks each day and check for lice on a regular basis. Ask a grown up for help if you can.
- Take a bath or shower daily.
- Shampoo your hair at least every few days, and comb or brush out any tangles.
- If you feel sick, let a grown up know.
- Use deodorant if your armpits are starting to smell.
- Wash your hands before eating.
- Wash any cuts or grazes and put a Band-Aid on any open or bleeding sores.
- Wash clothes after wearing them, especially underwear and socks.

There are many more ways to keep your body clean and healthy—can you think of some?

_____

_____

_____

_____

_____

Create a comic strip using a Band-Aid as the main character.

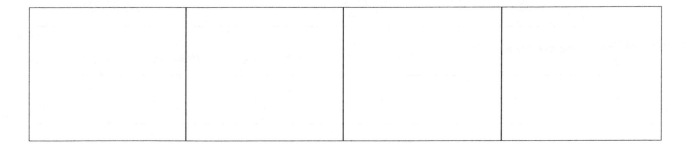

Part of taking good care of yourself is also knowing how to relax and calm yourself.

Draw a picture of a place where you feel calm.

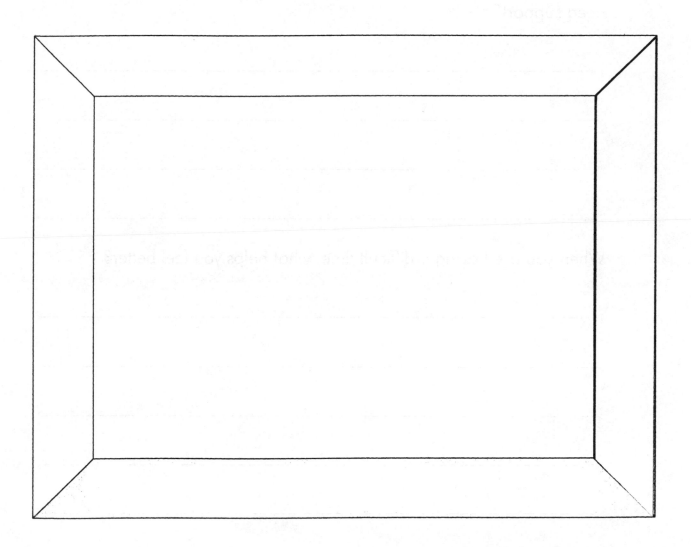

List some things that are calming to you.

_____

_____

_____

_____

Do you have a special friend or someone special you can turn to when you need support?

_____

_____

_____

_____

When you are having a difficult time, what helps you feel better?

_____

_____

_____

_____

Pick out a color you find soothing, then color or paste it here.

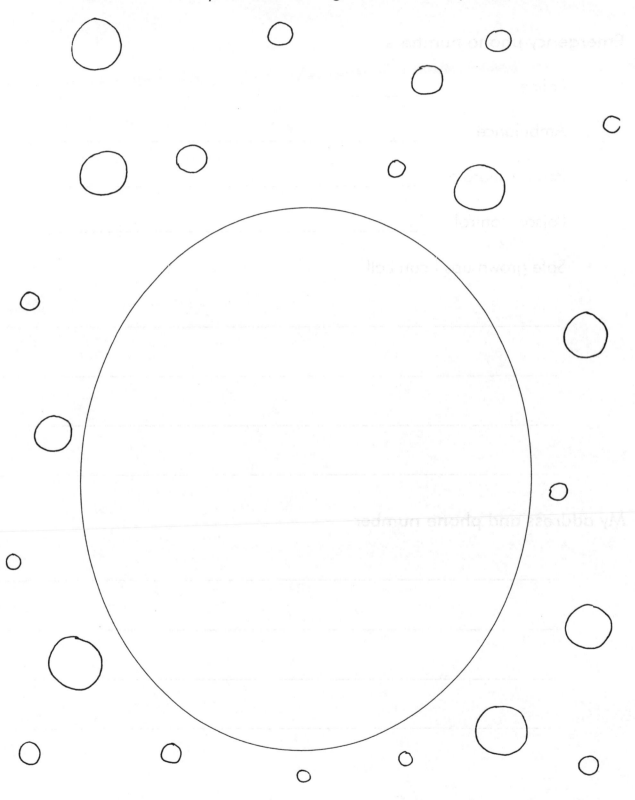

In case of emergency, it's always good to be prepared and know who to call.

Emergency phone numbers

Police _____

Ambulance _____

Parent/guardian _____

Poison control _____

Safe grown ups I can call

_____

_____

_____

_____

My address and phone number

_____

_____

_____

_____

My Action Plan

A healthy food I will try and eat more of _____

Something I will try to get a better night's sleep _____

A fun physical activity I can add to my day _____

A calming activity I can do when I need to relax or quiet my mind

_____

Safe grown ups I can talk to when I need support or have questions

_____

Wish Fairies

It is helpful for children to talk about their wishes because it gives the heart hope and it's healthy for children to know what they desire in life. Talk to children about what they wish for and listen with respect. Wishes sometimes even lend some insight into the child's inner world and needs.

Wish Fairies is a delightful activity—even the adults I have worked with have enjoyed it! Specific directions to make Wish Fairies follow.

Materials

- Wooden clothes pins
- Fabric scraps
- Embriodery string or yarn (for hair)
- Glue
- Permanent marker (for drawing facial features)
- Embellishments e.g. sequins (optional)

How to make wish fairies

- Cut a wishing strip of paper and write on it.
- Wrap your wish around your fairy's body.
- Glue the wish around your fairy's body.
- Glue the wish into place.
- Glue a piece of fabric around the fairy's body.
- Cut out rectangles for making the arms.
- Colour the rectangles and then roll them tightly.
- Tape the rolled paper so it doesn't unroll.
- Glue the arms onto the fairy and then draw a face onto the fairy.
- Choose the fairy's wings – colour and cut them out.
- Glue the wings onto the fairy's back.
- Glue any embellishments (sparkly stuff) onto the fairy.
- Create a crown or wand if you like!

Crowns you can decorate and cut out for your fairies.

Fairy arms:
Roll this way

Wishing strips

To make a wand cut these and roll tightly. Tape the paper into place so the wand does not unroll.

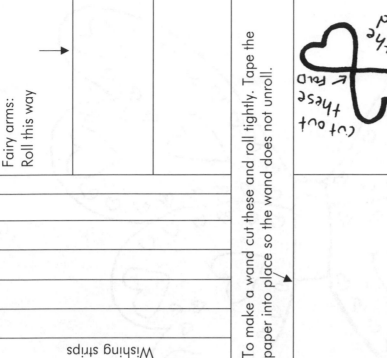

cut out these Fold

for the wand

for a flower wand

For a star wand

heart wand

Wishing Wands

Based on the same premise as the Wish Fairies, create a Wishing Wand to encourage a child to express their hopes and wishes.

Materials

- A dowel or stick
- Cardstock
- Scissors
- Markers or crayons
- Stickers
- Glue
- Glitter
- Ribbons

Directions

- Cut out two identical shapes for the top of the wand (e.g. two stars or two hearts).
- Have the child decorate the shapes with markers, crayons, stickers, and/or glitter.
- Glue the shapes to the tip of the wand—one on each side of the wand, back to back.
- Tie some pieces of ribbon together and then tie them to the tip of the wand.

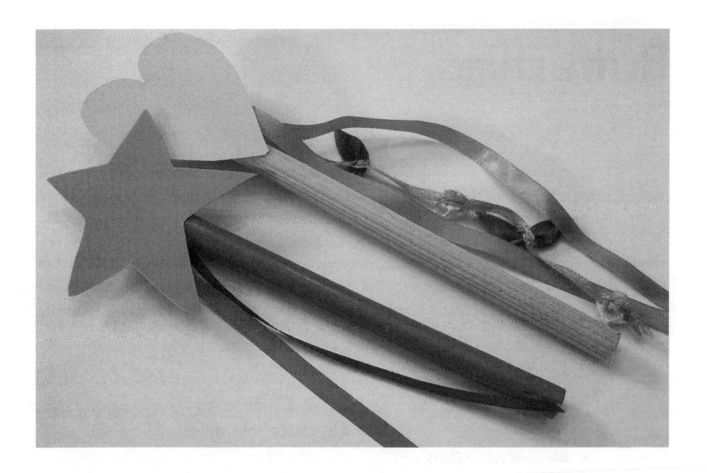

Butterflies

I like to make butterflies with children who may be lacking in confidence, who have low self-esteem, or children who are selectively mute. Butterflies are a wonderful metaphor for these children because they represent transformation. The stages of metamorphosis also provide metaphors that children relate to. Children with anxiety seem to relate to how safe and secure the caterpillar must feel in the chrysalis. They can easily project their feelings onto the butterfly by talking about what it will be like for the butterfly to leave the chrysalis and enter the world. These are wonderful talking points you can address while creating a butterfly with the child.

Materials

- Wooden clothespins (old fashioned type without the spring)
- Bleached coffee filters
- Water
- Watercolor paints
- Paintbrush
- Newspaper
- Permanent marker
- String (for hanging the butterfly)

Directions

- Place the newspaper down and set your materials on top.
- Give the child a coffee filter and let them paint a design on it with watercolors. As the child paints, the colors will spread through the filter.

- When the child is done, insert the diameter of the coffee filter into the clothespin and pull the filter up into the clothespin while shaping the wings on either side.

- Draw a face on the butterfly if desired.

- Tie a string onto the butterfly if the child would like to hang it somewhere.

- Allow the butterfly wings to dry—as they dry they will stiffen and stay in place more easily.

Snakes

Snakes need to "shed their skin" in order to grow and thrive—this is another metaphor children relate to in the face of change. Create these snakes with children as you talk about changes. What changes has the child experienced? Has the child ever moved? Changed schools? Changed teachers? What was it like to experience these changes? How did the child cope with change? What advice does the child have for another child experiencing change?

These snakes are wonderful decorations to hang in your home, office, or classroom. They spiral and turn in the wind and air—children love these!

Directions

- Have the child color the snake on the following page (photocopy the snake first if you are going to need more than one).

- Cut the snake out according to the directions on the page.

- Punch a hole in the snake's tail and tie a string through so the child can hang it (if the child is the type to be rough with it or swing it around, you will want to put tape or other strengthener around the hole or it will rip).

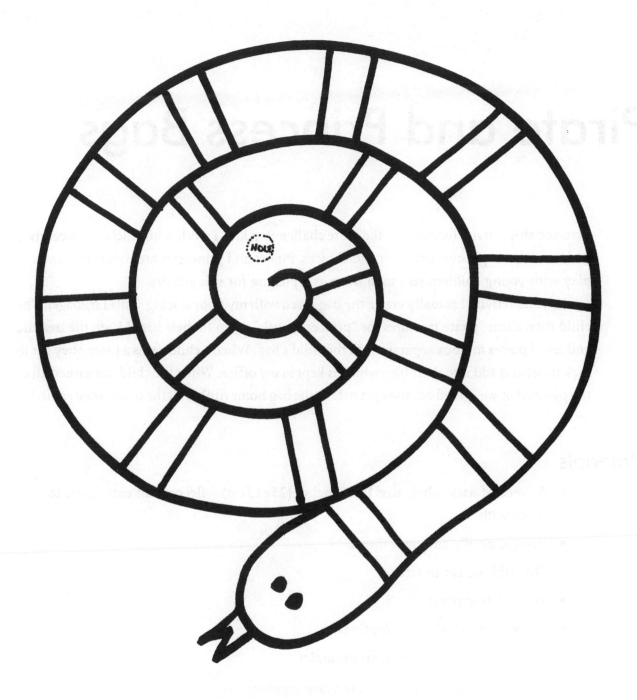

1. Colour the snake

2. Cut out the snake, following the black lines of the snake's body

3. Punch a hole where it says 'hole'

4. Tie a string through the hole

Pirate and Princess Bags

I created this activity for some of the more challenging kids I work with who need incentives and rewards for positive behavior and choices. Pirates and princesses are common themes in play with young children so I used them as a premise for this activity.

For this activity I actually create the bag (even with my poor sewing skills I manage). The child then earns "pirate treasures" or "princess jewels" to go in their bag. I keep the treasure and jewel pieces in a box separate from the child's bag. When a child earns a piece, they get to pick it out and add it to their bag, which is kept in my office. When the child has earned all of the pieces that we agreed on, they get to take the bag home (full of all the pieces they earned).

Materials

- A piece of dark fabric size 10x5 inches (25x13cm)—fleece is an easy fabric to work with

- Sewing needle and dark thread

- One ribbon, cut to size

- White fabric paint

- Sparkly embellishments (optional)

- Jewel and treasure pieces, for example:

  ○ Pretend gold coins (found in party supplies)

  ○ Real pennies

  ○ Glass gems and beads that look "real" (i.e. red gems look like rubies, green gems look like emeralds)

  ○ Pretend jewels and jewelry (found in party supplies)

o Faux pearl beads

o Plastic gold and silver beaded necklaces (found in party supplies)

Directions

- Fold your piece of fabric in half and sew along each side.

- Turn the bag inside out so that the seam is now hiding.

- Make three small cuts (about half an inch or 1cm) in the fabric along the top edge of the bag. Do this on each side of the bag.

- Weave the ribbon through these holes so you can tie the bag shut when needed.

- Use fabric paint to paint a skull and crossbones or princess crown onto the bag.

- Allow bag to dry.

Helping Children Manage Unstructured Time

Whatever your role is with a child, you will have heard the proverbial "I'm bored" and "Can I play my video game or watch TV?" Children seem to struggle with unstructured time these days. Coping with boredom is a skill children need to learn. Try to teach children early on to be creative with their time.

On the following pages, there are many ideas for activities that children can do with a few minutes of unstructured time.

Directions

- Cut out each of the ideas and put them in a container. You can fold, scrunch, or roll the strips of paper. You can even leave them flat.

- Provide the child with some enticing stickers and markers to decorate the container.

- The next time the child complains of being bored, gently guide them to the container and have them pick out an idea and try it.

If you have a child with a stubborn streak, or an emotional child, you can set some rules around using the container such as "You can watch TV after you have tried one idea from the container." And eventually you may be able to say "Try two ideas from the container before watching TV."

Get Your Scissors Ready!

Take off your socks and draw silly faces on your toes. Will any of your toes have a moustache? Eyeglasses? A curl of hair? A beard? Make up silly stories about your toes. Better yet, make up a musical. Sing up some silly stories and make those toes sing and dance! Give each toe a different voice—a baby voice or grumpy old man voice, or even a principal's voice. If you have a younger brother or sister this will make them giggle. If you have a dog or cat this will make them crazy and they may try to eat your toes, so be careful.

Find a piece of thick paper or thin cardboard (like from a cereal box). Cut out a person or animal and decorate it. Then you can use regular paper to make outfits for it, like a paper doll. Think this is just an activity for girls? Think again! Make a paper doll of your teacher. Then make outfits out of paper that are sure to make your teacher more interesting and exciting, like an instant alien outfit. (Did your teacher just grow eight arms? And an extra eyeball? Yikes!) Turn your younger brother or sister into a giant hairball with a giant hairball outfit! Turn your principal into a…into a… Ok, go get started now. Go make some paper/cardboard people and have some fun!

Turn a box into a diorama. Know what a diorama is? It's a 3D scene inside a box. Do you have matchboxes or little cars/trucks? Draw some muddy hills in the background and use play dough for hills that your cars can zoom over. Can you turn a box into a house for one of your dolls? What other worlds could you create inside a box?

Draw a family portrait—be creative with it. See if you can draw your family as building-block people...or aliens...or cartoon people...or superheroes...get the point? How many silly, crazy, outrageous family portraits can you make?

How many people in your family? Make a placemat for each person in your family. Will you make designs? Make puzzles? Draw pictures of their favorite things?

When you are all done, put the placemats on the table. Yay! When's dinner?

Create some bookmarks for your friends and family. Draw silly pictures on them, like an army of books stampeding a castle! Use your imagination and make some fun bookmarks.

Draw a knight and cut out pieces of aluminum foil or other shiny material (like the inside of a chip bag) to glue onto the knight's armor or shield. Make a prince and princess and use the same shiny material to make their crowns. Or make a dragon and use the shiny material to make really cool scales going up and down its back! You can also make fairy godmothers (use shiny material on the wand or wings), mermaids (shiny material for scales on her tail), or use shiny material on car parts you have drawn. Wow—shiny material is fun!

Have a grown up help you get a sheet of aluminum foil. Flatten it out on a table or other flat surface. Use a pencil to draw a picture on it—you won't see the pencil but the pencil will make cool lines in the aluminum foil.

Get some paper and pencils/markers/crayons. Draw a map of what your bedroom looks like so that when you are an old man or old lady, you will have a picture of your bedroom when you were little. Don't have a bedroom? Draw a picture of your dream bedroom!

Design some paper airplanes or other flying objects (you can use two paper plates stapled or glued together to make a spaceship). You can use aluminum foil or shiny paper (like from the inside of a chip or cookie bag) to add some really cool designs to them. Just don't fly them in the house if it's not ok with the grown up in charge. This will make them very grumpy, and grumpy grown ups are no fun! Maybe you can fly them outside if it's nice out.

Draw a comic strip using only pictures and the words "Oh no!" Later on you can share it with family and friends and have a good laugh! Laughing is good for you!

Make your own pirate map! Get a piece of paper and crumple it up really tight. Then flatten the paper and crumple it again a few times till the paper looks old and wrinkly. Then get a tea bag (black tea) and soak it in some warm water (too hot…you will burn yourself and that would be very sad). Squeeze the water out of the tea bag and then rub the tea bag over your paper. It will turn your paper brown and make it look very old. Let your paper dry before drawing a map on it. You can add some instructions on your map like "Look Out! Quicksand here!" or "Shark reef ahead" or "Friendly tribe here will trade bananas for silver" (this is *not* a good deal, by the way. But you knew that didn't you? Pirates are usually not very smart, and plenty have given up silver for fresh fruit). Add some palm trees and treacherous pathways and you have an instant pirate map. Don't forget—X marks the spot!

Create your own stationery! Get out paper, markers, crayons, and stickers…design some stationery for yourself or for someone else as a present!

Make some thumbprint people and animals! Color marker over your thumb and then press your thumb onto paper to make a thumbprint. Now add a face and silly details, like elf ears and whiskers and a pirate's moustache. How many different people can you make? Can you make a family portrait? Can you make a marching band? Circus performers? Invent some thumbprint cars and buses? Can you draw thumbprint pirates sword fighting? How many crazy pictures can you make from your thumbprint?

Put some fun stuff in an envelope for a relative and mail it to them—for example, send them some schoolwork you have finished (find a piece you are especially proud of); draw them a picture; make them a list of all the things you like about them; and then see if you have any stickers or confetti to put in the envelope. Don't have any confetti? Make your own—it's fun!

Make your own pretend money. Make enough to share with a brother, sister, or friend. Draw really silly faces on the bills.

Make a "lift the flap" picture. You will need two pieces of paper for this. On the first sheet of paper draw a picture such as a building with several windows or a store that has many bins inside (like a candy store or a hardware store). Once that picture is drawn, cut a flap over the spaces you want to peek at. For example, if you drew a window, you would cut out three sides of the window (the fourth side is the side that will be folded—don't cut all four sides). Cut all the flaps you will need to show what's behind all the windows or candy bins, etc. Now line up both sheets of paper keeping your drawing on top. Open the flaps and lightly trace with a pencil where the flap opens. Do this to all the flap areas. Now go to the second sheet of paper and fill those flap spaces with what you want. Is there a woman playing an electric guitar behind a window? Are there octopus gummies in the candy bin? Robot arms in the hardware bin? When all your flaps and pictures are done, carefully tape or glue the edges of the papers together. Now you can open the flaps and see inside!

How many zoo animals can you make out of paper? Can you make the animals stand up using folded paper or gluing them to little boxes? Make as many as you can and make a zoo. See if you can design their habitats using paper, play dough, rocks, or Popsicle sticks.

Find some dark paper and a white crayon. See how many of these pictures you can draw—four sheep ice-skating; a spooky ghostly picture; a snowy owl on an igloo; a skeleton drinking hot steamy tea; a great white shark chasing jellyfish; a snowman picking his nose; or a castle made of ice.

Draw a picture of something fluffy and then glue cotton balls over the fluffy parts. For example, use cotton balls for clouds or bunny tails or sheep.

You will need some white paper, crayons, and watercolor paints for this activity. Draw a picture on your paper with the crayons. Then paint over it with watercolor paints. Try different styles of pictures—for example, try drawing some dragonflies, color them with crayons, and then paint over it all with one color watercolor paint. Or draw a snowman on paper and then paint over it with blue watercolor paint and see the snowman "show up" out of the white paper. See what happens when you draw stars in a night sky and paint black or blue over it. Experiment and have fun!

Try drawing an upside down picture. Either draw a picture of something that is upside down (e.g. monkeys hanging upside down from a tree; someone bungee jumping; penguins sliding down a steep ice hill) or try to draw anything with your paper upside down—this means *you* are right side up and the *picture* is upside down.

Try drawing a self-portrait with your opposite hand.

Draw a picture made entirely from dots. This can take some patience so try a simple object to start with, like a flower or a car. If this seems too easy for you move on to a more challenging picture like a giant arthropod devouring shoppers in a department store.

Make your name in bubble letters and decorate each letter of your name in a different color or design (stars, hearts, lightning bolts, stripes, circles, peace signs, etc.).

You will need a pencil and some thick paper (index cards or cardboard from a cereal or pasta box). Cut out two circles of equal size (about the size of your fist). On one circle draw a picture of a fish bowl. On the other circle draw a fish (make sure your fish is drawn on the lower half of your circle). Now tape the circles onto the pencil so that the pictures are facing the outside (the fishbowl on one side and the fish on the other). Is it taped really well? Ok, now hold the pencil between your palms and rub back and forth—watch your fish bowl. Can you see the fish in the bowl?

Find some paper lunch bags. Decorate them with pictures, stickers, ribbons, markers, and anything else festive. Next time you need a gift bag for something small you will be prepared! You can even make your own shredded paper to fill the bottom of the bags—just cut up strips of paper (make sure they are thin strips) and crumple them up in your hands before putting them in the bags.

Design your own crown out of paper and attach it to a paper strip that is long enough to fit around your head (you may need to stick two pieces of paper together to make a long enough strip). You can put anything shiny on your crown like silver crayon designs, aluminum foil, or shiny material from a chip/cookie bag, or use beads and glitter if you have it. You can also make yourself a royal cape and a royal staff. Just don't *act* too royal (aka bossy) or your royal family will find it annoying and plot against you. If you want to rule a kingdom it's best to use your stuffed animals/dolls.

You will need a paper or plastic bowl for this activity. Draw a face on the bowl and then glue or tape several streamers, pieces of string, curly strips of paper, or ribbons all the way around the rim of the bowl. Voila! Instant jellyfish!

Make your own connect-the-dot pictures.

Create your own travel bingo boards so the next time you are in the car you can play travel bingo with a family member or friend! Take two sheets of paper. Draw a tic-tac-toe board on each. Then draw an object in each box—an object you will see while on the road. Some object ideas: a church; a school bus; a person waiting to cross the street; a dog; a playground; a grocery store; a gas station; a tree; a black car; a minivan; or a license plate from another state. Make sure the boards are different from each other. Next time you are in the car you can use the boards to play travel bingo. When you have found the object, just cross it off. The first person to find three in a row (like tic-tac-toe) wins the game!

Do you have circle-shaped cereal in the house? Make a necklace out of it and then eat it! Or make a necklace out of raw pasta, but don't eat it (that would be yucky).

Create a collage. Do you know what a collage is? A collage is a picture made from cut out pictures or words (i.e. from a magazine or newspaper) and other objects. For example, you could create a collage of your favorite things. You could draw some pictures of your favorite things…then look through a magazine and cut out pictures or words of *more* favorite things (ask a grown up if this is ok first—they may not want their magazines all cut up)…and then add some other items from your favorite things like a movie ticket stub or candy wrapper from a favorite candy. Arrange them all on a piece of paper and then glue them in place. Voila! A masterpiece!

Make some puppets. You can make puppets from old socks or paper bags and some markers. Or you can make paper puppets by drawing a picture of a character, cutting it out, and gluing it on a Popsicle stick. Think this sounds boring? Think again! Use your imagination to come up with some really cool characters—like a second-grader with night vision, or a fairy with hiccoughs. Create elaborate stories about good versus evil, cats versus dogs, or Silly T-Rex versus Grumpy Pterodactyl. Create a masterful scene and play it out for your friends and family!

Gather up some blankets and pillows and make a fort in your bedroom or living room (with a grown up's permission). Sometimes it's easiest to drape blankets over chairs to create walls and a ceiling. Once the fort is built, bring in a special stuffed animal and some books and maybe a flashlight if you need it. What else can you bring in the fort to make it feel cozy and fun? You can also come up with other names for your fort—is it a dragon's lair? A superhero's hideout? An office cubicle? A secret hideout from your brother or sister?

Gather up some teddy bears or favorite dolls or stuffed animals and have a teddy bear picnic in your house! Put a blanket on the floor and then put down some paper or toy plates (draw some on paper and cut them out if you need to) and pretend cups. If you have any pretend food you can put it on the blanket. If you don't have any pretend food you can draw some and cut it out. Enjoy the picnic and don't forget to use your best manners!

Build a fairy house! You can make fairy houses in every season. You can sculpt a little snow fort or snow house for your fairy in winter. Or you can make one out of sticks, rocks, shells, and leaves in the spring through fall. There are many ideas for fairy houses at the library (ask for books on fairy houses). Some places in Maine in the United States have whole fairy communities or neighborhoods! See if your friends want to build a fairy house next to yours! After you build the house, look for signs that fairies have been visiting!

Do you know how to whistle yet? If you don't, now is a good time to practice! Whistling is sometimes best learned on your own, so take some time and experiment! Already know how to whistle? Then see if you can whistle these songs—a theme song from a TV show; the Happy Birthday song; or make up your own song about the bionic princesses versus the slimy green vegetables (this will require some very dramatic whistling so it's for experts only).

Make mailboxes for people in your home—you can make some out of boxes or you can just make "mail pockets" out of paper. Make one for yourself and each person who lives in your home. When you want to talk to someone at home and they are busy or not home, you can write to them and tell them what's on your mind. Put the message in their mailbox and they can read it later. This works great for times when, for example, the grown up in your house is busy on the phone…or if there is something you want to talk about with them but it's hard to talk about it and you would rather write it. Or just write them a note about how much you love them. Maybe you will even get some mail back!

Any special events or holidays coming up? Make a paper chain to count down the days! For example, if it's 121 days till your birthday, make a paper chain with 121 links in it (this means you will need to cut 121 strips of paper). How many days till Halloween? How many days till summer vacation? Each day you can take one (and only one) link off the paper chain. This will show you how many days left till your special day!

Get a piece of paper (or many pieces of paper) and draw a road on it. Draw buildings, parks, or shops along the roads. If you have any play cars or toy people, you can put them in your new town!

Pretend your house is really a fancy hotel! Quietly go around the house and make everyone's bed. Then find a small treat you can leave on everyone's pillow (make sure if you have little kids or pets at home, that the treat is safe—no chocolate if there are dogs in the house, nothing small enough to choke on if there is a toddler). Go into the bathroom(s) and fold down the edge of the toilet paper into a V shape. What else can you do to make your house look like a fancy hotel?

Using odds and ends around the house, see how many types of ramps you can build for a toy car in your home—which ramp makes the car go further? Faster? What's the longest ramp you can make? If you don't have a toy car you can use a marble or something else that rolls. But do not use a brother or sister, no matter how roly-poly they are.

Make a marble-zip-around by using boxes and toilet paper rolls and other stuff from around the house. See how long a path you can make for a marble to follow. Can you make a curve? A bridge? A hole for it to drop through?

Make a glass of ice water for a grown up in your house. Tell that person to put their feet up and to relax while you go clean your room. Ok, so this one isn't very fun for *you*, but it sure will be fun to see the look of surprise on their face. But really, go clean your room. Put some music on and make it fun. Grown ups need a break now and then.

Make a house of cards! Clear a space on the table or floor. Get a deck of cards and see if you can make a house. If you have many decks of cards, ask a grown up if you can have one deck to make into *special* house-building cards—to make these cards, you cut a small slit at the center of each side of the card. Then you can slide the cards into each other using the slits!

Make your own treasure chest—find a box in the house you can use (ask a grown up first). You can cover the box in paper and decorate it, or you can paint it (if you have paint and a grown up says it is ok). While the treasure chest is drying, go around the house and see what shiny things you can put inside. You can cover bottle caps with aluminum foil to make silver coins...or cut out coins from cardboard and cover them with aluminum foil (or color them with markers). Are there any pennies under the couch cushions? Can you make some fake pirate money?

Do you have any dominoes in the house? See how many dominoes you can line up and then knock the first one and watch them all fall. Here are some challenges—use some props around your house (like a book) to see if you can make dominoes go up a ramp...or around a corner...or in two different directions!

Be an undercover super-secret chore doer—see if you can trick the grown up(s) in your house by doing a chore you are allowed to do (but do it secretly). For example, say the grown up in your house is busy on the computer... See if you can sneak into the kitchen and sweep the floor without anyone seeing you. Did anyone see you? If not, see how many of these chores you can do without being "caught." If no one notices right away, see how long it takes for someone to say "hey, wait a minute...something looks different here!" And see the funny look on their face if they can't figure it out. However, if they *do* figure it out, they will still have funny face when they realize that, whoa! Wait a minute...*You* did a chore without being asked? What? See the look of complete and utter confusion come over them! Now *that's* entertainment!

Do you have jigsaw puzzles at your house? Try and do a puzzle with the pieces upside down or completely flipped over (with the white side showing). Or, create your own puzzle! Draw a picture and then cut it into pieces and see if you can put it back together.

Make a fishing or crane game. For a fishing game you draw and cut out fish from thick paper or thin cardboard (like from a cereal box). Attach a paper clip to each fish. Then tie a magnet to the end of a string and see how many fish you can catch using the magnet! Or, if you have metal nuts and bolts and paper clips around, pretend you are a crane and swing the string with the magnet over the "junkyard" to collect all the scrap metal.

Find a toilet paper tube or paper-towel tube to create something—will you make a kaleidoscope? A telescope? A tunnel for your pet hamster? Binoculars? A tunnel for a toy car? A spy scope? A castle turret? What will it be?

Make some sock balls or paper balls. Get a laundry basket and see how many balls you can throw into the basket…or put an item on the floor and see how many times you can hit it with the sock/paper balls. Just don't use a brother or sister as a target no matter how pesky they are.

Make a rubber band ball! Start with a pile of rubber bands. If you don't have a lot of rubber bands then ask a grown up to get you some and then put this idea back in the jar till you have some. To make the rubber band ball it may help to start with a marble or superball at the center to make wrapping rubber bands around the ball easier. Just keep wrapping rubber bands around the ball in even layers and in different directions till it is the size of a ball.

Make a paper clip necklace. Of course, you need a lot of paper clips to do this, so go look and see if you have any paper clips. If you don't, then put this idea back in the jar or throw it away. If you do have paper clips, make a necklace by linking the paper clips together. Or you can make a chain for something else—does a toy car need a tow line? Do your knights need chains for the dungeon? Get creative!

Does your doll or stuffed animal have clothes? If so, create a clothesline for the clothes and pretend to have a "wash day." Pretend to wash the clothes. Then drape the clothes over the clothesline or hang them with clothespins. Later you can fold the clothes and put them in a "basket" (have a basket or box around to use as a laundry basket).

Gather some pencils from around your house. Make silly pencil toppers for them using googly eyes, pipe cleaners, or just plain paper—see what funny pencil toppers you can create and then put the new and improved pencils back where you found them. The next person who needs a pencil will be surprised!

Get a pencil and paper and create your own comic strip where you are the superhero and you create your own villains. (Are the villains giant man-eating sunflowers? Are the villains eight-headed aliens from the Icky Gooey planetoid called "Blah"?) Go ahead, make up some crazy comics!

Make your own Zen garden—you will need about a cup of sand, a few rocks, and a plate. Ask a grown up if there is a plate you can use for this project. If not, you can use a paper plate if it has a rim or you can use a shoe-box lid. Fill the bottom of the plate or lid with a layer of sand. Then use a fork to make lines in the sand—any design in the sand will do. Now place some stones or rocks in the sand. There you have it—an instant Zen garden. Don't let your brother eat it.

Create a home for an insect. Find a little box, plate, or flat container. Put a piece of lettuce or piece of apple in it. See if you can find a ladybug in your home or a spider. See if it would like to visit for a little while in your new insect home—just don't shut it in or it could die. Just let it explore in your home and let it leave when it wants.

Make a plan for the ultimate sleepover party. Who would come? What would you do for fun activities? What foods would you eat?

Create a teddy bear clinic (doctor's office). You can also make a doll clinic, a superhero clinic, etc. First you will need a comfy spot, like a cot or bed, for your patients. Then gather up all the clinic stuff you can find, like some Q-tips, Band-Aids, cotton balls, and toilet paper (for gauze). If you have a toy doctor's kit you can use that also. Now go take care of all those broken bones and boo-boos!

Create a book for your younger brother/sister/cousin (take about six pieces of paper and fold the pile in half to make a book). What will it be about?? Maybe you can make it about their favorite stuffed animal—what adventures will it have? Maybe you can write a bedtime book to help them go to sleep at night.

Design your own dream menu for the week, or even just one day. Mmmm, ice cream anyone?

Create an alphabet book (take 13 pieces of paper and fold the pile in half to make the book). Come up with a picture for each letter of the alphabet. You can even choose a theme for the book if you are feeling really ambitious. For example, could you do an entire alphabet book on dogs (C is for Collie, D is for Dachshund, etc.)? On sports words (S is for "Strike one," T is for "Time out," U is for "Underhand," etc.)? Go ahead—give it a try!

Make a list of all the things you want to do when you are a grown up. Design your own dream house, draw your dream car, set some outrageous goals for yourself (I will be the ruler of the world! I will be a triple trillionaire! I will own 1000 chihuahuas!) This is your list—have fun with it!

Make a birthday card for someone. Make many! Set them aside for when a family member or friend has a birthday. Maybe you can even put them in a special box until you need them.

Write a letter or postcard to someone, even if they live next door—tell them all about your day or tell them a funny joke! Make sure you have the right address on it. Ask a grown up for a stamp and mail it!

Create your own joke book (take six pieces of paper and fold them in half to make a book). Write all the jokes you know inside!

Create the ultimate birthday party! Will there be a theme (race car party, spa party, tea party, etc.)? Who will come? Where will the party be? What will you eat?

List all your favorite things—favorite places to go, favorite people, favorite movies, favorite snacks, etc.

Write a thank you letter or thank you note to someone who has done something nice for you lately. Did a friend help make your day more fun? Did a grown up help you solve a problem? It's never too late to send someone a "Thank you"!

Make a list of all your favorite pet names.

Create your own word find puzzle with one of these themes: Football; Bubblegum flavors; Local street names.

Write out plans for The Best Day Ever. How will your day start? Who will be a part of this amazingly fun day? How will the day end?

Make someone a card—tell that person how much you appreciate them.

Create your own recipes for your favorite foods. Put a bunch of them together in a cookbook or just write out one recipe and see how close you come to the real thing. For example, write a recipe for how you think brownies are made (without using a store bought mix). Then look up a recipe for brownies in a cookbook and see how close you came. Yum!

Create your own tongue twisters and write them down. See if anyone can say them later.

Create your own word find puzzle with the theme: Candy.

Write your own scavenger hunt list—make an indoor list and an outdoor list. Then do the scavenger hunt with a parent, friend, or brother/sister. Here are some ideas for an indoor scavenger hunt—find something soft, a dirty sock, a dust bunny, something that starts with the letter R, something round, something from inside the couch cushions…get the idea? Make as many lists as you can—that way you can play many different times!

Write a letter to your president or prime minister stating what you want to see changed in this country or in this world. Make sure you let the president know how old you are and why these issues are important to you and this country/world. Put it in an envelope with a stamp and the address. For example:

President _____ of the United States

The White House

1600 Pennsylvania Avenue NW

Washington, DC 20500

Create a restaurant play set. First, take a long-sleeve shirt and tie it around your waist backwards. This will look like a waiter's/waitress's apron. Then find some paper and make an "order pad." Write "Orders" across the top. Find some toy plates and cups, or some paper plates. Set up a table or blanket with a pretend table setting. Next, make your menu. You can put whatever food you want on the menu, just make sure the prices are *outrageously* high. Ask a brother or sister to be a customer...or if no one is willing, you can use some stuffed animals.

Make up your own game. Get a large sheet of thick paper or some cardboard (like from a cereal box). Draw the shape of the board you want and mark off a pathway around the board. Section off the pathway and now you can create your game! Look around your house for playing pieces. You can use coins, buttons, small rubber insects, or small plastic dinosaurs...anything small enough to fit in your squares will do. Cut up some paper into card shapes and create cards for your game (e.g. "go ahead 5 spaces" or "you lose a turn" or "jump ahead 3 spaces and do a dance"). You get the picture now don't you? Go create a fun game and see who is brave enough to play it with you later.

Make up your own secret code you can share with a friend.

Create your own dinner conversation cards. Cut up some paper into small card shapes or use index cards. Write some questions on the cards that would be fun to talk about over dinner or family time. For example, here are some sample questions: Name three things that make you happy; Tell us about a time you helped someone out; What is your dream car?; What is your favorite holiday and why?; Tell us a story about a time you laughed really really hard. Now make a pile of these cards and bring them to dinner or a family gathering. Take turns reading questions to each other and answering them.

Part 2

Specific Interventions for
Worried Children

Worry Dolls

Worry dolls are a wonderful intervention for children and have been around for years! Children can whisper their worries to the worry dolls and the dolls will hold onto the worries for them. You can always purchase worry dolls but the kids I work with love to make their own!

Materials

- Wooden clothespins (not the type with the metal)
- Scrap fabric
- Scrap yarn or string
- Low temp glue gun and glue sticks
- Small sticks, pipe cleaners, or tightly rolled papers for the arms
- Permanent marker (to draw a face)
- Embellishments if desired (sequins or pretend jewels)

Directions

- Choose a clothespin to be the doll's body.
- Cut out a piece of scrap fabric and glue it around the doll's body. You can also wrap yarn or embroidery string around the body for clothing.
- Next, create the arms. Some children prefer pipe cleaners—I just snip the pieces we need and glue them on. Other children have preferred tiny sticks or Popsicle sticks broken to size. You can also use tightly rolled paper for arms.
- Next, cut some yarn for the doll's hair. I usually cut several strands about the length of the doll's body. Gather the strings and tie one more string around the

center. Now you can glue this knot onto the doll's head and this will secure her hair in place.

- Draw a face on your worry doll.

The worry doll is now complete! At any time the child can whisper his or her worries to the doll and the doll will hold onto those worries for the child.

Worry Warriors

If the child is looking for something fierce to fight off their worries, you can make another version of worry dolls, called worry warriors. Worry warriors help children to visualize their worries being fought and kept at bay.

Materials

- Wooden clothespins
- Scrap fabric
- Scrap yarn or string
- Low temp glue gun and glue sticks
- Small sticks, pipe cleaners, or tightly rolled papers for the arms
- Scrap paper
- Aluminum foil
- Permanent marker (to draw a face)
- Scrap cardboard

Directions

- Cut a piece of scrap fabric to be your warrior's cloth or armor. You can even wrap your warrior in aluminum foil if you want armor that's really shiny. Glue and wrap the material around the clothespin.

- Find some scrap paper or aluminum foil to tightly roll into "arms." Cut arms into desired shape and glue onto sides of warrior.

- Glue some yarn or string onto head if hair is desired. You can also construct a helmet out of paper and glue into place.

- Draw the facial features.

- Create a sword and shield out of cardboard and then cover with aluminum foil. I also prefer using shiny, textured paint samples (from the hardware store) for this part of the project to add some fun detail.

- Glue sword and shield onto warrior's hands.

The child can visualize the warrior helping to fight off their worries, or shielding them from their worries.

The Worry Dragon

Sometimes it helps children to visualize their worries as one entity, especially if they are chronic worriers. If the child can visualize their worries as an entity, then they can practice various visualizations for defeating it. In this activity the child will visualize their worries as a dragon.

Details to consider

- How many heads does the dragon have?
- Does it fly?
- Does it have scales, lumps, and bumps or is the skin smooth?
- How big is it?
- Can it swim?
- How fast can it run?
- Does it have a name?
- What powers does it have?

If the child is feeling creative and wants to take it a step further, have them create an image of their dragon (i.e. draw, paint, scribble, or make a stick figure of it). If the child feels completely devoid of artistic talent you can always print an image off the internet for them to color or collage over.

Ask the child to visualize him- or herself standing in front of the dragon. You can even suggest "Imagine it is trying to scare you with every power it has. Imagine yourself standing strong before it, not falling prey to any of its tricks and intimidations."

Protection Shield

Now that the child has created their dragon, they need to make a shield to protect them from it and their worries. This can be a creative process in that they can choose any size shield they desire, as long as you have the materials for it. I have worked with children who have made teeny tiny shields that we turned into pins so they can be worn (we simply hot glued a pin to the back—but the child needs to be able to attach and remove the pin safely). Other children have wanted shields to be larger and more durable for play or decoration. Your materials may vary but below is a basic list of supplies.

Materials

- Cardstock or cardboard for the shield (e.g. a recycled cereal box)
- Paints, markers, or crayons
- Scissors
- Metallic paint or aluminum foil if you want a shiny shield
- Scrap metal for decorating (i.e. grommets, washers, nuts and bolts) but only if you have a strong shield that can hold these
- Low temperature glue gun and glue sticks, or other adhesive
- Other items for decoration, for example a coloring page downloaded from the internet with either a symbol or mythical creature (like a *fluer-de-lis* or unicorn); glass gems from a dollar store; stencils; stickers.

Directions

- Draw or trace a shield shape onto the cardstock or cardboard.
- Cut out the shield.

- Cover the shield with paint or paper to provide a nice backdrop for the child's artistic expression.

- Have the child visualize their worry dragon and imagine what sort of shield will help protect them from this dragon and their worries. For example, what personal strengths do they have or what personal resources do they use that help them cope when they are feeling worried? Together, think of how the child can symbolize these strengths and resources on the shield. A lion might represent courage, for example, or a sun symbol may represent how calm they feel when at the beach.

- The child can glue on any symbols, pictures, or embellishments and allow the shield to dry.

Hang the shield in a place where the child can be reminded of their strengths and resources that help them combat their worries and keep them at bay.

Dream Catchers

Dream catchers are a classic activity for children who have nighttime worries and/or scary dreams. Dream catchers are created to hang safely over a child's bed. The dream catcher captures the bad dreams in its web so they can't reach the child. They can be made in so many ways, but the instructions below give the overall gist of how to construct one.

Materials

- A ring made from durable material—you can cut a ring from a plastic lid (like from an oatmeal box or coffee can); cut one out of cardboard; or create one by bending a metal coat hanger into a ring shape (this is better left to older children as my experience has been that coat hangers are stubborn about being bent into a ring)
- Yarn, twine, or waxed string
- Shells with holes in them and/or beads
- Other natural embellishments such as a feather or a small picture of a power animal

Directions

- To create the dream catcher 'web' tie one end of a long piece of string onto your ring.
- Tie seven–nine hitch knots around the ring, spacing them evenly apart. Keep the string taut when going from one knot to the next.
- To start the next row of the web, begin tying hitch knots in the middle of the string loops already completed. Continue tying hitch knots in the same way until you are satisfied with the shape and design of the web.

- To complete the web, tie a double knot in the string and trim off any excess.

- At the bottom of your dream catcher tie three pieces of string hanging down. Attach any beads or embellishments to these strings and tie them so they stay on.

Hang the dream catcher over the child's bed or place of sleep and make sure it is hung safely.

Worry Vacations

It can be helpful for a child to use their imagination to "visualize" their worries going elsewhere for a bit so that they can take a breather and just be a kid. Here are some simple visualizations that take only seconds for children to imagine.

- Imagine you are lying outside someplace safe and comfortable. You are lying back, watching clouds pass slowly by. Each time you think of a worry or have a worry thought, send it up into the sky and onto one of these clouds. Watch the worry float away on the cloud.

- Imagine you are at a dock and the worry ship is about to depart. Imagine your worries donning their sunglasses and carrying their luggage onto this ship, as they prepare to take a vacation elsewhere for a bit. As your worries find their way onto the ship's deck, wave goodbye to them and watch as the ship starts to pull away from the dock and sail away to sea.

- Imagine your worries have decided to take a rather long trip to outer space. Visualize your worries putting on their space helmets and space uniforms as they board the shuttle for some distant planet. When it's time for the countdown, imagine yourself saying goodbye to your worries and count down 10, 9, 8, 7, 6, 5, 4, 3, 2, 1…blast-off!

- Imagine your worries sitting on the Lost and Found table at your school. Picture yourself passing by them in the hallway and deciding not to reclaim them.

- Imagine your worries at the local library. Your worries and worry thoughts can be pretty noisy and bothersome can't they? Imagine all of those worries at the library being "shooshed" by the librarians.

- Imagine all of your worries going on a submarine. Picture the submarine slowly moving out to sea and then submerging into the ocean waters.

- Imagine "breaking up" with your worries. Tell each worry or worry thought the reason why it doesn't contribute to a better life for you and that you are done with it.

Some children will create humorous visualizations of their own and this can be a fun activity in and of itself, to think of all the ways you can "send the worries away." Make a silly game of it—where did the worries go?

Take this activity a step further by having the child draw the scene of how the worries departed. Or, have the child write their worries a postcard wishing them well on their vacation.

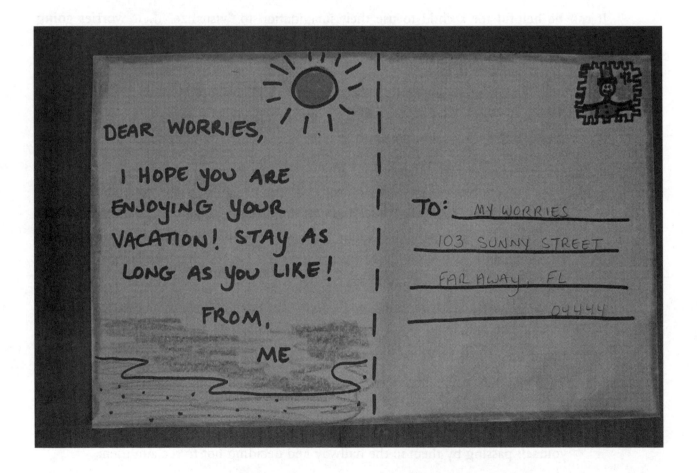

The Worry Wall

If you work with many children, a worry wall can be an ongoing activity. The worry wall is a place where children can express their worries anonymously.

Materials

- A large piece of white paper (how large this paper is will depend on the availability of wall space you have and/or the size of envelopes you use for this project)
- 20 red envelopes (to start with)
- Tape
- Paper and writing utensils

Directions

- Tape the white paper to your wall space.
- Let the children you work with know that this is temporarily a worry wall. Explain that you have red envelopes which will be the bricks in the wall. Anytime the children have a worry they want added to the wall, they can write or draw it on a piece of paper and then put their worry in a red envelope. They can seal the envelope and tape it to the wall in a brick pattern. Children seem to like the idea that (1) they get to express their worries and (2) they get to do so anonymously.

As the wall becomes more decorated it also becomes a visual to show children that everyone has worries, not just them. Sometimes children feel better just knowing that worrying is part of being human and they are not alone.

Worry Pizza

This is a useful exercise for understanding the scope of issues your child/client is worrying about, and is a great visual for the child.

Directions

- Let the child list the things they worry about (if they have a zillion worries then have them categorize them).
- Next have them divide these worries into at least three categories such as "worry a lot about this;" "sometimes worry about this;" and "worry a little bit about this."
- Next, draw a circle.
- Divide the circle into ratios of how much space each worry takes up—yes, this takes a little math and forethought.
- If the child chooses, they can decorate the "pizza" while talking about their thoughts on how their worries were proportioned (e.g. "Mom being in the hospital is a very big slice of pizza—it takes up almost the whole pie").

Take this activity one step further by allowing the child to use stuffed animals or puppets to act out eating up this worry pizza—what happens to them when they eat it?

Time Out

Find a regular time each day for the child to visualize putting their worries aside for a designated amount of time. For example, each day at 5pm get the child to imagine putting their worries in time out, and to picture all those worries sitting in time out chairs or on a bottom step.

Take this one step further by actually creating a doll or stuffed animal and give it a worry name (e.g. The Infamous Mrs. Worry). Then the child can put the actual doll in time out.

Hope and Prayer Flags

Prayer flags are a beautiful expression of people's hopes and prayers in times of struggle. Children can make their own prayer flags by decorating squares of muslin cloth with their hopes and wishes, or prayers. The flags are hung clothesline-style along a string and then hung in the wind where the breeze will carry the hopes and prayers to heaven. This activity is especially nice when done in a group setting (such as with a support group or with a family) as it can be a wonderful visual to see all the flags hung together. Or, one child who has many worries can make their own chain of prayer flags. Any child who is worried and/or facing extremely difficult challenges may feel some release putting their worries into action.

Materials

- Muslin cloth (or any solid color fabric), cut into 6x6 inch squares
- Fabric paints or permanent markers
- Twine or other durable string
- Safety pins or glue

Directions

- Have each child choose at least one square of cloth.
- Encourage the child to think of a worry they have and then to think of a positive outcome they would like to see happen or a prayer they would like to express.
- For those children who know what prayers are and are comfortable with the term "prayer," they can actually write out their prayers as they would in their own religion. If the child does not come from a particular religious or spiritual practice (or the child is too young to write yet) they can express their desired outcome with a picture or statement of hope.

- Gather a long piece of string or twine and attach the flags to it with safety pins or glue. If using glue you will need to fold over the top part of the flag and glue the flag over the string.

- When the prayer flags are hung and dry, find a place outdoors where they can be strung in the breeze.

Part 3

Specific Interventions for Grieving Children

Memory Stones

Memory stones are cement memorials created specifically for a loved one who has passed. You can buy kits for this activity but it's less expensive to make your own. Depending on the age and maturity of the child, you may need to do much of this project on your own. At the very least, you can have the child participate in this project by letting them gather some durable mementos, stones, or glass baubles for the design.

Materials

- Cement mix (you can get this from a hardware store)
- Bucket for mixing cement
- Rubber gloves and a mask for safety
- Something disposable to stir the cement (e.g. a paint stirrer)
- A plastic mold for the cement (you can buy these at a hardware store but you can be creative and use recyclables such as a bowl/plate from the salad bar or line an old pan or sturdy cardboard box with plastic wrap or a garbage bag)
- Durable trinkets or items about the person/pet/loss (no paper items)
- Either a pointed utensil (e.g. the pointed end of a paintbrush) or store-bought letter molds made for cement—these are used for writing on the memory stone
- Newspaper

Directions

- Gather your trinkets and items ahead of time. For example, for a pet's memory stone you may use such items as: the tag from their collar; a piece of their fur; a small toy they loved to play with; pet-themed buttons from a craft store; medium-large heart-shaped buttons or beads.

- Prepare for cement making—lay out the newspaper someplace level. Get your gloves and mask on and prepare for a fun but messy project.

- Follow the directions for mixing the cement according to the cement bag. Pour or scoop cement into your plastic mold. Again, if you have decided to use an old pan or even a sturdy cardboard box, make sure every part of it is sealed in plastic, such as a garbage bag.

- Set the cement in the mold someplace level. Jiggle the mold slightly to allow the air bubbles to surface and for the cement to settle. If you are using cement with rocks in it, this will also help the stones to settle to the bottom of the mold, leaving a smoother surface for your memory stone.

- If water settles at the top of the memory stone you can dab it with paper towels.

- When cement starts to congeal you can start decorating your stone. Do your lettering first, such as the person/pet's name. Then add your items/mementos around it. Make sure any objects you push into the cement are pushed in well enough to stay put but also visible.

- Allow the stone to dry and "cure" according to the directions on the cement bag. If this stone is going to be walked on, such as in a garden, then give the stone ample time to cure otherwise it will crack under the weight of people's feet.

Now the stone is done! When it is cured you can place it outside in a special area. If you enjoy making these stones, you can make an entire path leading to a special quiet space where you can go and remember your special person/pet/loss. You can also place the stone at the bottom of a tree or plant that you have planted in their memory.

Mini Memory Garden

Sometimes children get sad when a person or pet is buried in a place they can't visit too often. With a mini memory garden you plant one garden at the place where a loved one is buried/memorialized and you plant one garden at your own place. Both gardens are identical. When *your* garden starts to bloom and grow, the child knows the other garden is also blooming and growing. It's a nice connection for the child.

This project requires that you are able to visit that place (i.e. cemetery) at least one more time or that a family member or friend is able to visit it for you and do some planting.

Directions

- Gather a few plants that will grow where this person/pet is buried. You want to buy double of what you plan for because you will be planting one mini garden for yourself and one for your loved one that passed.

- You can either grow your mini gardens in pots (if you are likely to move anytime soon) or plant them directly in the ground.

When your plants are blooming or going into dormancy, you will be able to envision the mini garden at your other location doing the same. When my son was grieving the loss of a family friend, he planted spring bulbs at our friend's cemetery plot and the same spring bulbs in a special location in our yard. Each spring when the crocuses start to poke through the snow and start blooming, we imagine the crocuses at our friend's plot blooming as well. It is a pleasant and peaceful reminder of our friend.

Memory Shrine

Memory shrines are display boxes filled with photos and mementos of someone who has passed, or something near and dear the child has lost (such as a house in a house fire). The child collects mementos and photos that remind them of what/who was lost and they assemble them in a box that can be displayed.

Materials

- A small box—this can anything from a bought box from a craft store (made of papier mâché or wood) or a sturdy recyclable box
- Paints or paper to cover the box
- Collected memory items to put in the box, for example:
  - A favorite recipe from that person
  - A candy wrapper from a candy they enjoyed
  - A ticket from an event the child went to with that person
  - A photo of that person, place, or pet
  - Any picture or object that reminds the child of him/her/it
- Adhesives such as regular glue, hot glue, and/or PVA glue

Directions

- Cover the interior and exterior of the box with paper or paint. This will give the shrine a nice backdrop for decorating.
- When the glue and/or paint has dried, start gluing the memory items into the box. The child can assemble these items however they desire.

- When the shrine is all decorated and complete, hang it on the child's wall or place it somewhere special. You can even use recycled mint tins and matchboxes to make "pocket shrines"!

Nana enjoyed many activities and passions depicted in this shrine—Bingo, rose gardening, feeding backyard birds, baking oatmeal cookies, and going to performances at the local theater. Some of Nana's items from her sewing supplies were also added, including ribbon and buttons.

A Memory Candle

When a special person or pet dies they can be especially missed on special occasions and holidays. To remember missed loved ones on these occasions, have a special candle that is lit in their memory or as a reminder of them. This can be a nice tradition or ritual for children. The candle is lit and put somewhere safe but central to the occasion. To take this ritual one step further, create a special candle holder for the event.

Candleholder ideas

- Use crafting clay to create your own custom-made candle holder.

- Purchase a wooden candle holder to decorate—make sure it has the metal insert for fire safety. Wood can be an inventive medium as you can découpage it, paint it, and glue items onto it.

- Purchase a plain glass candle holder and use glass paints and simulated liquid leading to design another custom-made candle holder.

- Try the classic PVA glue and tissue paper design. You will need a glass candle holder, tissue paper, and PVA glue. Tear the tissue into little pieces. Glue the pieces onto the glass candle holder.

As with any candle holder, make sure the base of it is sturdy and that, above all, it is safe.

Messages to Heaven

Purchase one helium balloon per person. You and each participant can write a message to the person/pet/place that is missed. Tie the messages to the balloons and then tie the balloons to a safe spot till everyone is done. Release all the balloons together.

Sewn Memory Creations

When a special person passes, there is no doubt they can leave behind plenty of clothing that can be difficult to let go of. You can turn the person's clothing (and even linens) into several types of creations. Even if you are not handy with a sewing machine or needle and thread, perhaps a family member or friend is. Otherwise, seek out a professional to facilitate the project. It is worth the time and effort!

- Make a "stuffy" for a little one who is grieving. Choose a soft piece of clothing and design your own stuffed doll or animal. The child will have a special item to snuggle with when missing their loved one.

- Make a pillow out of the person's favorite T-shirt.

- If the person had a collection of ties, you can create a pillow or a seat cushion by connecting and sewing the ties together. The ties in the picture are now part of a little boy's pillow.

- Create a quilt from the person's T-shirt collection (some people may have a collection of sports team T-shirts, college T-shirts, environmental causes T-shirts, etc.).

- Create a quilt from various pieces of clothing that you particularly enjoyed.

- Remove labels from men's or women's clothing and then sew them together to create a small change purse or evening purse.

- Use old linens to create handkerchiefs, napkins, or sachets as gifts at a little girl's tea party or family reunion.

Of course, the more material you have the more you can create. Any of these items make great gifts for others who are grieving the same person.

Prayer Flags: Part 2

These prayer flags are specific to grieving. A group of children who have suffered a loss as a group (such as the loss of a teacher, community helper, or peer in their class) can benefit from this activity. Find a window or special place outside where the flags can carry messages of love and loss to the person who has passed on. See pages 153–154 for instructions.

My Little Book about a Big Loss

Here is an activity book for children who have lost someone special. You and the child can pick and choose which pages you want to add to your book. Cut out the pages you want and staple them together. The child can fill in the blanks and illustrate the book about their loved one.

My Little Book about a Big Loss

Created by:

_____

In memory of:

_____

_____

A special person/pet has passed away.

Their name was:

_____

_____

Here is a picture of them:

What I miss about them is:

_____

_____

_____

_____

_____

_____

_____

_____

_____

_____

_____

_____

_____

When I see:

_____

_____

_____

_____

_____

_____

_____

_____

_____

_____

_____

_____

It reminds me of them.

When I hear:

_____

_____

_____

_____

_____

_____

_____

_____

_____

_____

_____

_____

It reminds me of them.

When I smell:

_____

_____

_____

_____

_____

_____

_____

_____

_____

_____

_____

It reminds me of them.

Something they taught me:

_____

_____

_____

_____

_____

_____

_____

_____

_____

_____

_____

_____

_____

A funny moment we shared:

_____

_____

_____

_____

_____

_____

_____

_____

_____

_____

_____

_____

_____

_____

My favorite memory of them:

_____

_____

_____

_____

_____

_____

_____

_____

_____

_____

_____

_____

_____

_____

I feel thankful they were in my life because:

_____

_____

_____

_____

_____

_____

_____

_____

_____

_____

_____

_____

_____

Other people I know who are missing this person/pet:

_____

_____

_____

_____

_____

_____

_____

_____

_____

_____

_____

_____

_____

_____

This is a picture of how I feel:

People I can talk to about my loss:

_____

_____

_____

_____

_____

_____

_____

_____

_____

_____

_____

_____

_____

What I will do to take care of myself when I feel sad:

1. _____

_____

_____

2. _____

_____

_____

3. _____

_____

_____

4. _____

_____

_____

5. _____

_____

_____

She/he had a special talent:

_____

_____

_____

_____

_____

_____

_____

_____

_____

_____

Something they did that I thought was amazing:

_____

_____

_____

_____

_____

_____

_____

_____

_____

_____

_____

_____

_____

This is how long I knew him/her:

_____

_____

_____

_____

_____

_____

_____

_____

_____

_____

_____

_____

A picture of you

and me!

You and Me

I Miss You So Much

✓

The Stomp Box

Children can have a tough time managing the anger, guilt, and isolation that accompanies grief. The Stomp Box is a great activity to help the child express and release some of these complicated feelings.

Materials

- A recycled box (such as a cereal box—don't choose a box that is too sturdy or the child can twist an ankle stomping it)
- Several pieces of paper
- Writing utensils

Directions

- Let the child know, first and foremost, that when faced with a loss, each person experiences and feels it differently. It is important for children to know that their feelings, no matter how strange to them, are most likely normal human responses. It is ok to feel anger, sadness, fury, etc. at the loved one that passed, as well as dearly miss them.

- Have the child write or draw their various thoughts and feelings onto the papers. You can assist with the writing if the child is ok with you doing so.

- Remind the child, if needed, that absolutely every thought or feeling is ok to write or draw.

- The child can use as many pieces of paper as they need.

- Put all the papers into the box.

- When the child is ready, let them stomp on the box with all their might!